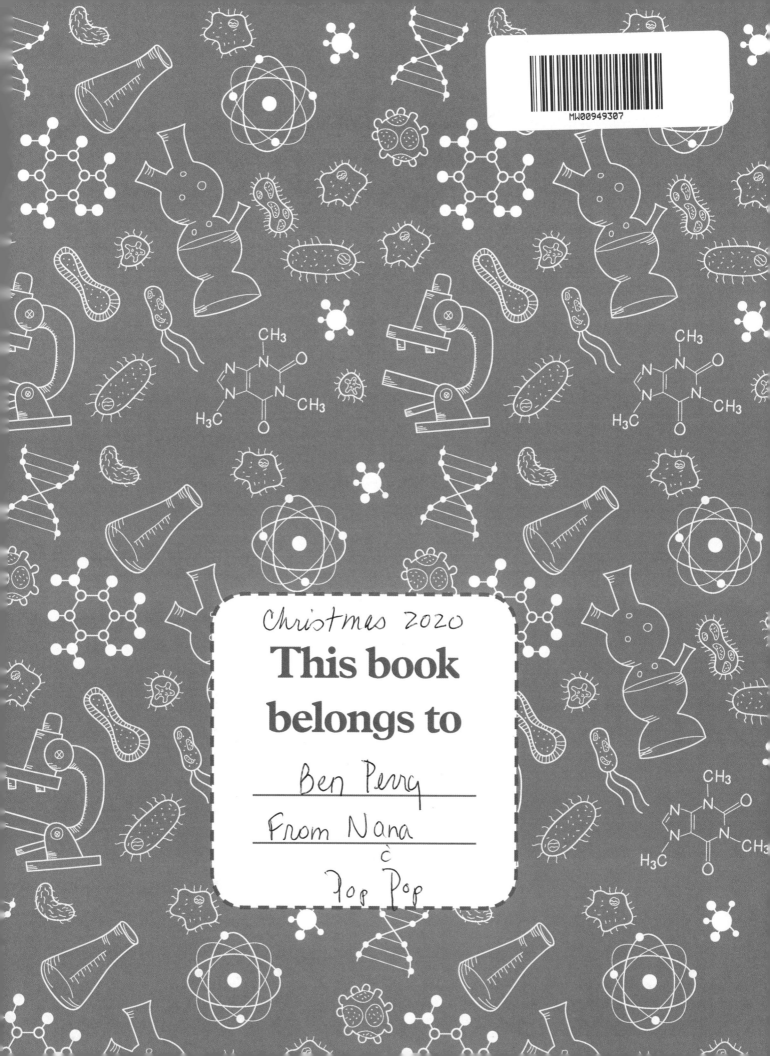

Christmas 2020

This book belongs to

Ben Perry

From Nana
c̄
Pop Pop

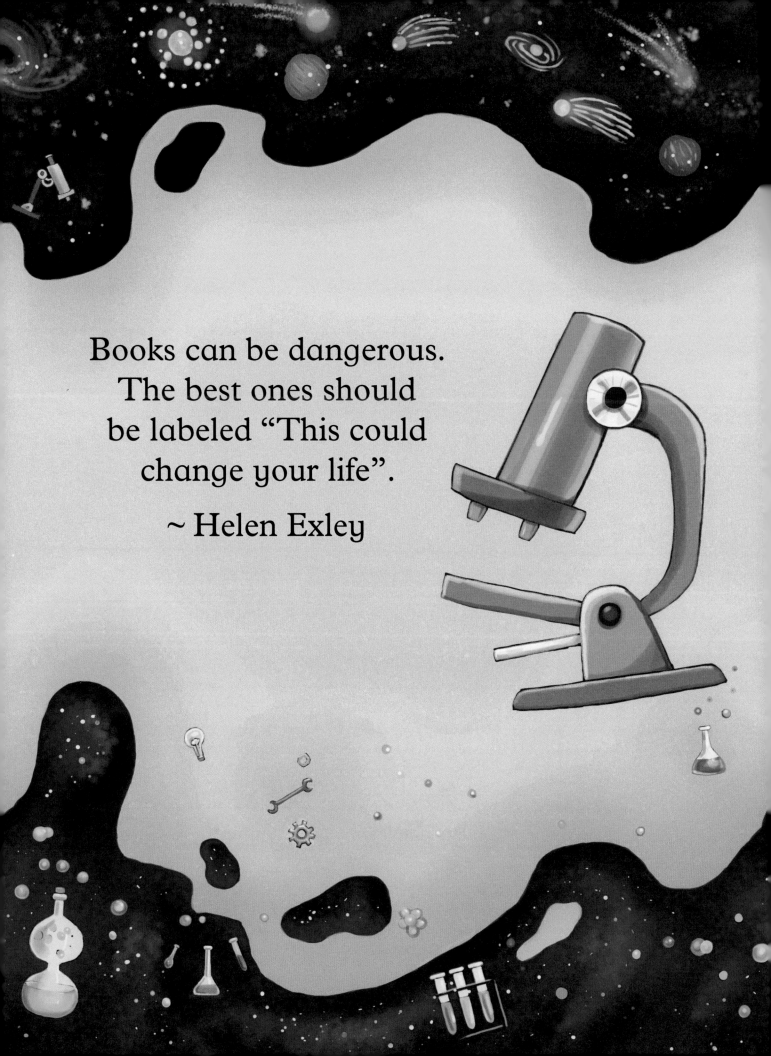

Books can be dangerous.
The best ones should
be labeled "This could
change your life".

~ Helen Exley

THE KIDS WHO CHANGED THE WORLD

$E=mc^2$

10 AMAZING SCIENCE STORIES

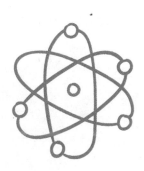

ISBN 9798676704704

Cover design by Anastasia Ermolina
Illustrations: Leyre Ramos Castro and Anastasia Ermolina

"I really had a lot of dreams when I was a kid, and I think a great deal of that grew out of the fact that I had a chance to read a lot".
~ Bill Gates

"A child who reads will be an adult who thinks".
~ Author Unknown

"Today a reader, tomorrow a leader".
~ W. Fusselman

• CONTENTS •

Message to the child:

How do you choose your steps in life?

Now look again from left to right,

Can you spot the difference between the two?

You think it's hard? Here is a clue!

Both boys were born in the same world

And then everything swirled,

The different path that one boy took,

All started from an open book!

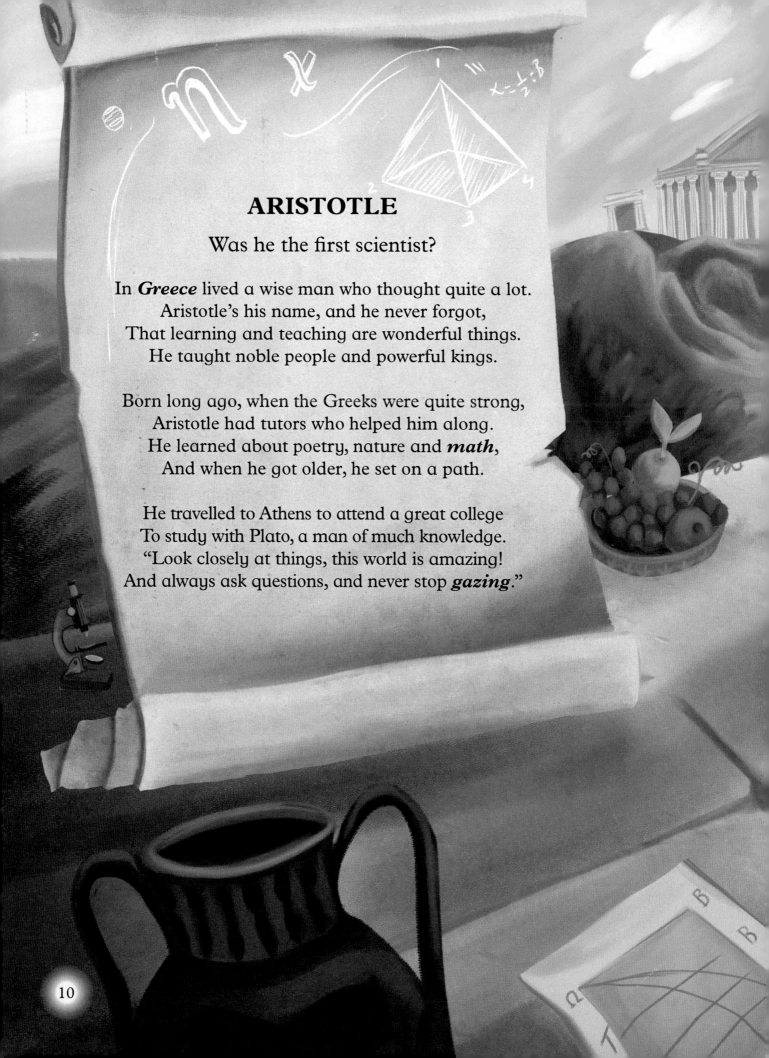

ARISTOTLE

Was he the first scientist?

In **Greece** lived a wise man who thought quite a lot.
Aristotle's his name, and he never forgot,
That learning and teaching are wonderful things.
He taught noble people and powerful kings.

Born long ago, when the Greeks were quite strong,
Aristotle had tutors who helped him along.
He learned about poetry, nature and **math**,
And when he got older, he set on a path.

He travelled to Athens to attend a great college
To study with Plato, a man of much knowledge.
"Look closely at things, this world is amazing!
And always ask questions, and never stop **gazing**."

He traveled a lot through Greece, coast to coast,
And found out that science was what he loved most.
He wrote about fish, and land animals too,
If he had the time, he could open a zoo!

Aristotle became a world-famous *scholar*.
And one day, King Philip gave him a *holler*.
"Aristotle, I want you to be our teenage son's teacher,
His name's Alexander and he's quite a smart creature."

Aristotle taught Alex about all kinds of stuff
Philosophy and logic, these subjects were tough!
Alexander loved school and learned to debate.
Today we all know him as Alexander the Great.

And when Alex turned twenty,
He did something cool
He gave Aristotle some money,
So he can open a school.
He gave it a name and called it
"Lyceum" (lay-see-uhm)
It had a library, gardens
And a fancy museum.

His students would learn
While their teacher spoke,
They'd listen, ask questions,
And sometimes they'd joke.
He told them that science
Is a wonderful quest,
And searching for knowledge
Is for the best.

Aristotle was special,
One of the best to exist!
Some people say
He was the first scientist!
He had a great life,
He was a wise man!
So, let's try to be like him
And learn all we can!

15

GALILEO GALILEI
Was Galileo right about the Earth?

Galileo Galilei was born
In Pisa, Italy in 1564.
His family worked hard,
But they were very poor.

Young Galileo was
A very happy boy.
Spending time with his father,
Filled his heart with much joy.

His father was a **composer**,
Well-known in Italy.
He wrote beautiful music
And played the **lute** skillfully.

Galileo became an accomplished lutenist himself,
But he was more interested in the books on the shelf.
So he went to a **monastery** to study in 1574.
To learn math, physics, **astrology** and much more.

Galileo's father wanted him to be a doctor someday.
So he sent him to The University of Pisa one day.
But Galileo really wasn't interested in medicine.
The sky and the stars were what he was interested in.

So he invented an improved telescope in 1609.
His new tool magnified things up to 20 times!
This telescope seemed to bring the objects nearer.
So he could see the planets and stars much clearer.

Galileo counted four moons around Jupiter.
And more stars than everyone thought that there were.
When he looked at Saturn he saw interesting things
The planet Saturn is surrounded by some rings!

Galileo was amazed by all that he could see.
His new telescope was a really great discovery!
When he heard of a famous scholar called Aristotle one day.
Galilei wanted to hear what he had to say.

But some things Aristotle said didn't seem right.
Galileo thought about it every day, every night.
He disagreed with Aristotle's law of *gravity*.
This made many people very unhappy!

Aristotle said a heavy object falls faster than a light one.
And his theory was accepted by almost everyone.
But Galileo didn't think that made sense at all.
So he went to the top of a tower and let two objects fall.

They hit the ground at the same time so Galileo knew,
That heavy objects don't fall faster than light objects do.
During that time people thought that it's right
To think that the Earth is at the center of the night,

They also thought that everything spins around us.
For Galileo, this subject was worth to discuss.
He thought that the Earth spins around the Sun
And proving his idea to everyone was such fun!

Experiment with things, and try with all your heart!
Be a great thinker, there's no better time to start!

ISAAC NEWTON

What is gravity?

Isaac Newton was born on Christmas day.
In 1642, on a farm, in **England**, far away.
As a small child, he loved making inventions.
Building **sundials** always caught his attention.

But he couldn't go to school, because his own mother,
Wanted him to be a farmer, just like his father.
Isaac hated the farming, working wasn't a thrill.
And to prove that he is smart, he build a windmill.

He went back to school and proved to everyone,
That doing what you love is always much more fun.
Isaac loved **math**, **physics**, and **astronomy**.

So at eighteen he went to Cambridge University.
One day, when Isaac was *gazing* up at the sky,
An apple fell down from a branch, way up high.
The apple hit him on top of his head.
Why didn't it fall on an angle, but straight
down instead?

He went to his house and started to study.
When he figured it out, he told everybody!
"There is a great force, that we all cannot see.
I decided to name it, it's called *gravity*!"

Gravity is always pulling everything down.
It keeps people and things attached to the ground.
This was Newton's greatest discovery!
But he wasn't scared to solve the next mystery.

There were so many things, he wanted to discover.
And also many mysteries, he wanted to uncover.

Some other discoveries that Isaac found,
Were things that would affect everybody around.
Like the laws of motion — one, two, and three.
And all the colors of the rainbows that we see.
Isaac invented a reflecting telescope too.
Now when looking at planets, we have a better view.

His laws of motion are still used today,
When rockets blast off and fly far away.
Isaac taught Math at **Oxford school** too.
His ideas were interesting, exciting, and new!

His students always said, "Tell me, more!"
They had never heard these ideas before.
One day Isaac Newton met Queen Anne.
She wanted to meet this intelligent man.

She came and laid a sword upon his shoulder.
This is how Sir Isaac received his title of honour.

MICHAEL FARADAY

Does reading make you smart?

In the English town of Newington Butts
A child was born inside a **hut**.
His dad was poor, a **blacksmith** by trade,
He earned a living from the things that he made.

28

The year was 1791.
Michael was the name of the blacksmith's son.
No money for books, and because of that rule,
Michael could not attempt a real school.

When he was 14, Michael found a job.
He sold books in a small, local bookshop.
He loved selling books, he enjoyed it indeed,
Mostly because now he had what to read.

Faraday had to educate himself,
And read everything, on every bookshelf.
He read a lot, I think you'll agree,
His brain became as full as it can be.

Then Michael met a chemist - Humphry Davy.
And became his assistant in chemistry.
He gave him access to his work and much more.
Now Faraday had a lot to explore.

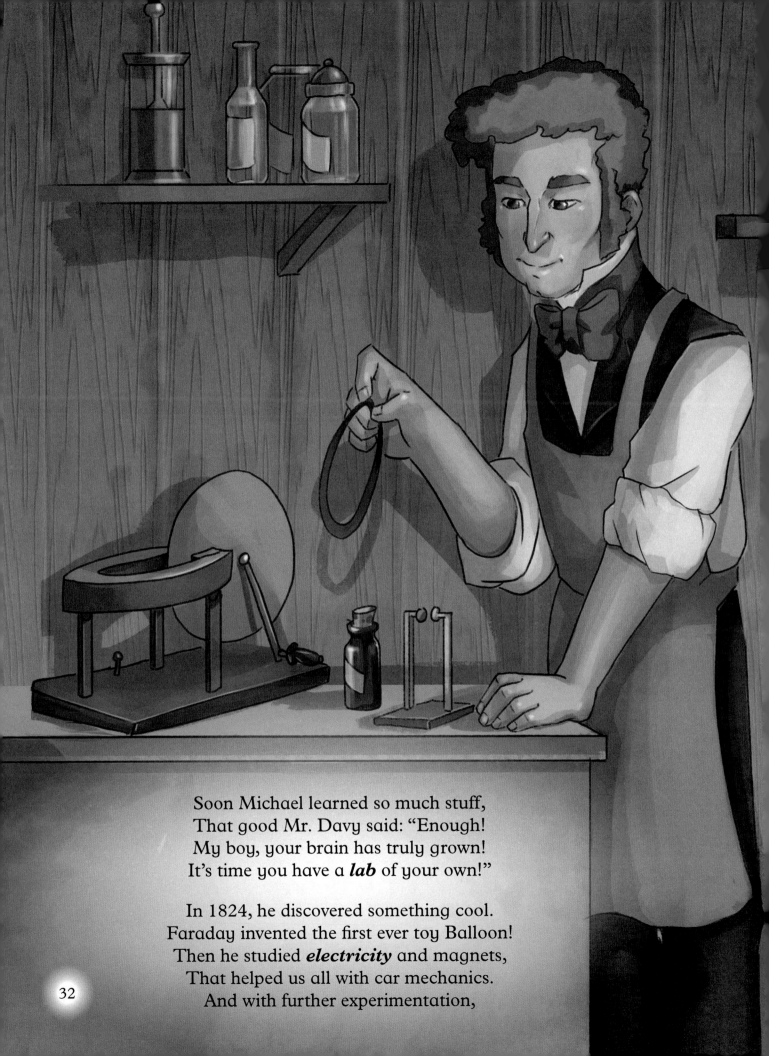

Soon Michael learned so much stuff,
That good Mr. Davy said: "Enough!
My boy, your brain has truly grown!
It's time you have a *lab* of your own!"

In 1824, he discovered something cool.
Faraday invented the first ever toy Balloon!
Then he studied *electricity* and magnets,
That helped us all with car mechanics.
And with further experimentation,

He discovered the **electromagnetic** rotation,
This was a very important discovery
For the future of science and technology.

He also learned how to make things cold.
That's why we have refrigerators. That's what I was told!
Now, Michael Faraday shows us how to succeed.
You open a book and read, and read.

It doesn't matter who you really are.
It's what you know, that makes you a star!

CHARLES DARWIN

What is the theory of Evolution?

So what is the *Theory of Evolution*?
It's what Charles Darwin's big contribution
To science was, way back before people knew
Where life comes from. Yes – even you!

He was born long ago, back in 1809,
The 5th of 6 kids in fair England's sunshine!
When he was a kid, he thought that nature was cool.
He enjoyed learning, but he didn't like school.

He took long walks in the woods every day.
And he collected insects as he went on his way.
He liked to do experiments to figure things out.
Because by *exploring* you become smarter, no doubt!

When Charles was older he went to medical school, but
He almost passed out at the *sight* of a cut.
He said, "I guess being a doctor isn't for me,
So when I grow up, what will I be?"

In 1831 Charles Darwin went on a trip.
He traveled the world on his famous big ship.
The ship was called The Beagle and it would be,
His place for fun adventures and new discovery!

Charles collected worms, beetles, shellfish, and bugs,
And took great pleasure in finding spiders and grubs.
He found the bones of a monster that was 14 feet high,
And he wrote about the Rhea, a bird that can't fly.

But the wonders that interested him the most,
Were found on the islands called Galapagos.
There were giant tortoises, the biggest to be found.
And lizards that can swim and crawl on the ground.

Each island was a little different, Charlie discovered,
But that wasn't the only odd thing he uncovered.
The creatures on each island were almost the same.
Little things were different, but they had the same name.

All living things looked different a long time ago...
He studied until one day he shouted, "I know!
The birds had changed on their own little *isle*,
So they could live in their very own style!"

They changed over time so they could stay alive.
They had to change or they wouldn't survive!
Darwin was happy he had found a solution.
He called his idea the ***Theory of Evolution***.

His ***research*** explains how life on Earth began,
From insects and birds to the women and men.
Charles wrote his ideas in a big book.
You can find it in the library. Now, go take a look!

LOUIS PASTEUR

What keeps milk fresh?

Have you heard of a thing called *pasteurization*?
It keeps milk fresh, and calls for a celebration!
Its inventor, of course, was Louis Pasteur,
Who heated things up, just enough to stay pure.

But how did this Louis know just what to do?
He conducted experiments – more than a few!
His discoveries not only help milk stay fresh,
But help us stay healthy and get sick much less!

A long time ago, Louis grew up in **France**,
And back then, people believed that you don't have a chance
If you get sick, then your sickness had to stay in,
Right there inside, where it had to begin.

But was that really true? Louis thought it was not.
Louis thought about it, and he thought a whole lot.
Louis thought hard, and with imagination,
He came up with something brand new: *vaccination*!

He proved that if given a weaker *disease*,
Someone could avoid a much bigger sneeze!
By giving someone a sickness real small,
Then after, that sickness would not come at all!

As a young student, Louis was not very special,
But his paintings and drawings were very successful!
He went on to study both science and art.
And each of those studies he loved with deep to heart.

Louis became a chemist and a **bacteriologist**,
And worked hard. He saw what some scientists missed.
Did he care that some scientists laughed at him?
No! Louis knew, his ideas would win.

Louis Pasteur is the Father of **Germ Theory**,
He helped us all understand it more clearly.
Without his discoveries, what would we do?
We would get sick more often, that's true!

44

Our milk, cheese, and juices would go bad much faster.
Without Louis, dinner might be a disaster!
The idea you have, with which no one agrees,
May be as small as a germ or as fast as a bee.

If you have a theory that no one believes,
Think like Louis and you will prove what you see!

JAMES CLERK MAXWELL

Is hard work the key to success?

James Clerk Maxwell was born in Scotland in 1831.
And like all little boys, he liked to play and have fun.
James was very curious and he loved to explore.
He asked many questions, so he could learn more!

When James was ten, he went to Edinburgh Academy,
Where he became very interested in **geometry**.
He wrote a scientific paper when he was fourteen.
Such a paper, from such a young boy had never been seen!

In 1850 James went to Cambridge University.
He continued to study science and geometry.
But because he was very curious about so many things,
He got very interested in the **Saturn**'s rings.

He discovered that the rings were not solid at all.
They are made of many pieces, that are all very small.
James loved to study *electricity*, *magnetism* and light.
His experiments would tell him if his theories were right.

James figured out how electricity and magnetism behaves.
The invisible power traveled through space as waves.
The discovery of the way *electromagnetic* waves form,
Led to the invention of radio, television, and even the phone!

He developed a set of *equations* to explain what he knew.
Maxwell's Equations were very exciting and new!
James was also fascinated by all the colors that we see.
This interest helped him invent color photography.

He used the colors red, green and blue in a new way.
The first color photograph was born on that day!
He also worked to help the colorblind.
This shows that his heart was as big as his mind!

James was a great scientist. That is very true!
His discoveries changed the world for me and you.
Although James was a quiet man and he didn't seek fame,
The tallest mountain on *Venus* was given his name.

Next time you really want to solve a mystery,
You know – hard work and dedication is the key!

NIKOLA TESLA

Who invented the first electronic device?

Nikola Tesla was a smart boy, and very curious too.
He knew that being an engineer, was what he wanted to do.
He loved math and science, and liked inventing things.
Once, he even made a motor powered by *June bug* wings!

Nikola Tesla also had a very big imagination,
If he could imagine it, he could turn it into an invention.
He was fascinated by the world and loved to discover.

All the mysteries of the world he wanted to uncover.
When asked what is his favorite thing, he scratched his head.
"Of all things I liked books best!" - Nikola Tesla said.
In 1884 He came to the United States with a plan.
His hero was **Thomas Edison**. He wanted to meet this man.

When they met, Edison was impressed right away.
He decided to hire Nikola to work for him starting that day.
But when Edison wouldn't pay him, Nikola became really mad.
That's where things between them started to get really bad.

They argued a lot, sometimes hours or days.
And at last they agreed to go their separate ways.
Tesla had many ideas that led to inventions.
One of them was the *wireless* communication.

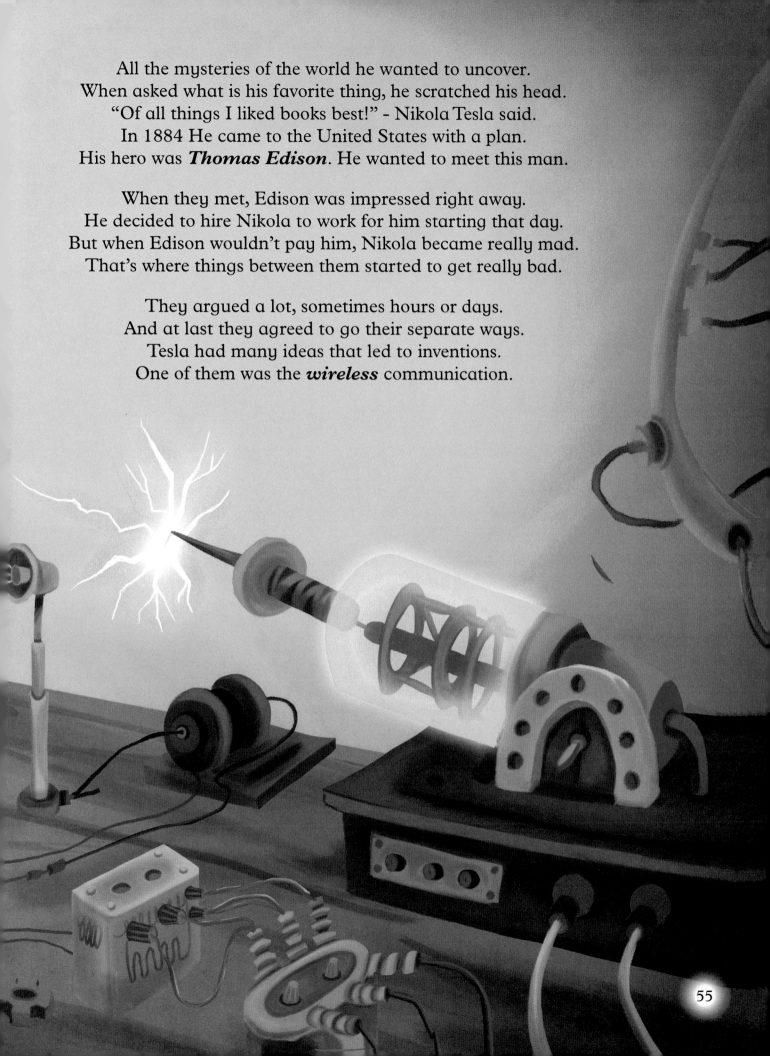

He was involved in making robots and remote controls.
Also an *X-ray* device was one of his goals.
He invented the **Tesla Coil** and with it you can see,
Beautiful flying arcs of electrical energy.

We use it for electrical lighting and X-rays.
And the Coil was used as a radio back in the days.
Nikola didn't sleep much. He worked hard every day.
To develop the current that powers our homes in a way.

This invention allows us to power the entire nation.
All because Nikola Tesla used his great imagination!
Do you have great imagination? I really hope you do!
The next great invention could be invented by you!

57

MARIE CURIE

How an X-ray can change our lives?

What is an **X-ray**? It shows us stuff that our eyes can't see.
Like bones inside our body. Who invented it? Marie Curie.
She was born in a country called Poland, you see,
She had curious eyes and her hair was quite curly.
Her parents were teachers, so she learned easily.

They taught her to read and write very early.
In Poland, back then, no girls went to college.
It was illegal, no matter their knowledge.

But in Paris, she could, so she travelled to France
And was quickly accepted, they gave her a chance!
After only three years, Marie earned her degree
In physics, a science she loved endlessly.

Soon after, she married a man named Pierre.
He also loved physics, they had something to share.
Marie and Pierre worked together quite closely
And discovered some things, two elements mostly.

Both elements gave off radiation.
Polonium and **Radium** were quite a new sensation.
Radium was risky, but if used the right ways,
It could help cure cancer or take X-rays.

Marie became famous and to her surprise,
She and her husband won a very big prize.
The **Nobel prize**, the biggest they say.
Marie's the first lady to win it! Hooray!

And in 1911, she won it again!
The first person to win twice!
Quite shocking! Oh, man,
Years later, the first **World War** arrives.
Marie was determined to save many lives.

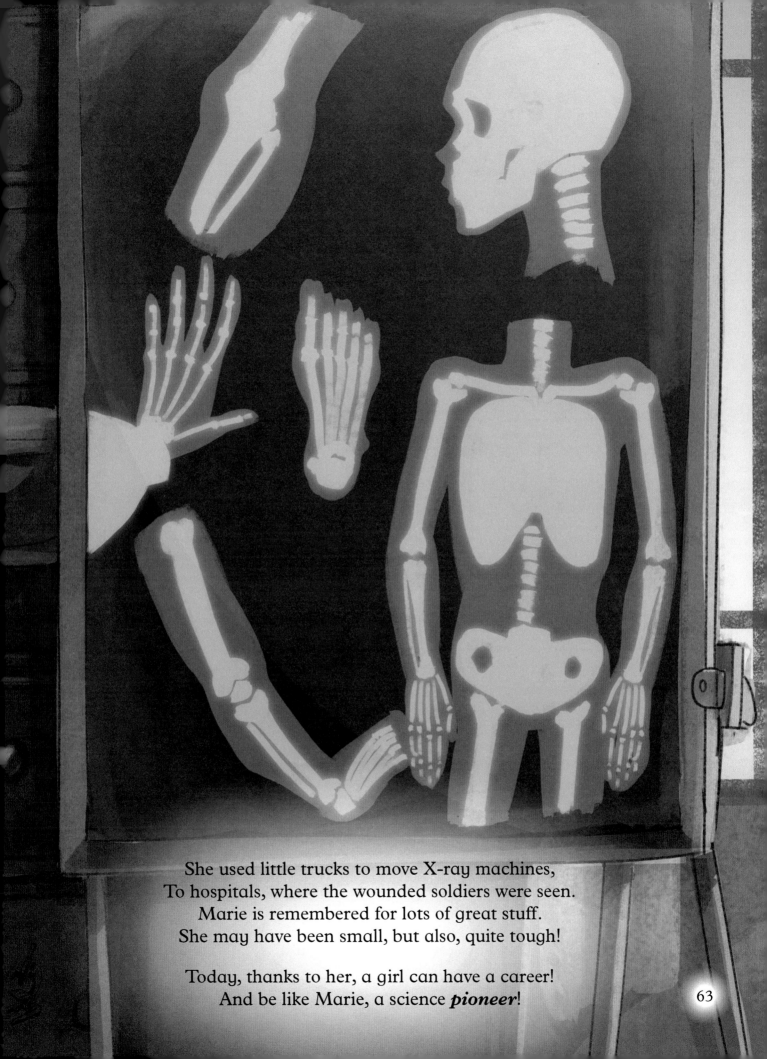

She used little trucks to move X-ray machines,
To hospitals, where the wounded soldiers were seen.
Marie is remembered for lots of great stuff.
She may have been small, but also, quite tough!

Today, thanks to her, a girl can have a career!
And be like Marie, a science *pioneer*!

ALBERT EINSTEIN

Can a little kid change the world?

Can the world be changed by one little boy?
Let me tell you a story that I know you will enjoy.
He was born in Germany on March 14th, in 1879.
But later moved to the USA, which turned out just fine.

When Albert Einstein was just a little boy.
His grandma bought him a special new toy.
It was a cool little **compass**. So shiny and new.
Beginning that day his love of science grew.

The kids at his school liked to tease him a lot.
Do you think that it bothered him? No, it did not.
Albert was a little careless, have you ever seen his hair?
He forgot to wear socks, I hope he remembered underwear!

Albert always knew that being different was ok.
He hoped those kids would find that out someday.
He loved learning so much, that he did it all by himself.
No school to help him learn, just his books on his shelf.

Even though, to him, some kids were mean,
He wrote a *famous paper* when he was 16.
As Albert grew up his imagination grew as well.
Then, one day, this quiet boy came out of his shell.

66

He had ideas that he wanted the world to hear.
He began to share his ideas with those far and near.
His ideas helped build spaceships and satellites too.
His inventions really changed the world for me and you.

He even came up with an idea. That was very wise!
It's called the *theory of relativity*, for which he won the **Nobel Prize**.
His idea is hard to understand, even for me,
Without Albert's idea, you wouldn't have a TV!

Albert loved the world and he loved people too.
If you were in need, he would always help you.
He loved to help people. His kindness had no end.
People who knew him said that he was a great friend.

Can a little boy change the world? Yes, he can!
This little boy grew up to be a great man!
So keep being curious about the world around you.
I know that someday you will change the world too!

• GLOSSARY •

ASTROLOGY – the science about the universe beyond the Earth's line

ASTRONOMY – the science about the celestial bodies and universe

BACTERIOLOGIST – a person whose job is to prevent, diagnose and prognose an illness

BLACKSMITH – a person who makes horseshoes and and other w objects out of iron

COMPASS – a tool that helps you tell the direction you are facing by using magnets

COMPOSER – a person who writes music

DISEASE – sickness

ELECTRICITY – a type of energy that we use to power lots of things around our homes. Electricity can be seen in nature in a bolt of lightning

ELECTROMAGNETIC – the phenomena associated with electric and magnetic fields and their interactions with each other

ENGLAND – is a country situated in Europe

EQUATION – a mathematical statement that two expressions are equal.

EXPLORING – to cross or walk on a land for the purpose of discovery or to look into something closely

FAMOUS PAPER – a scientific journal

FRANCE – a country situated in Europe

GAZING – looking steadily with great interest, pleasure or wonder

GEOMETRY – a branch of mathematics that deals with points, lines, angles, surfaces, shapes and solids

GERM THEORY – the theory that all contagious diseases are caused by microorganisms which are little germs too hard to see with your eye

GRAVITY – the force by which things tend to fall towards the center of the Earth

GREECE – a country situated in Europe

HOLLER – to shout or yell

HUT – a small and poor house that serves as a shelter

ISLE – a small island

JUNE BUG – type of insect, could be a firefly or beetle that appear late spring and early summer

LAB – a workplace for the conduct of scientific research

LUTE – a pear shaped musical instrument

MAGNETISM – a magnet is a rock or a piece of metal that can pull certain types
of metal toward itself. The force of magnets, called magnetism, is a basic force of nature,
like electricity and gravity

MATH – the science that studies and explains numbers, quantities, measurements, and the relations
between them

MONASTERY – a house or a place where people meet or live for religious purpose

NOBEL PRIZE – an annual award for outstanding achievement in science

OXFORD SCHOOL – one of the world's most famous and old schools. It is located in the town
of Oxford, England

PASTEURIZATION – a process that kills germs in food and drink, such as milk, juice,
can foods and others

PIONEER – a person who was a part of the beginning of something or one who led the
way for something

PHILOSOPHY – the study of why things are right and wrong

PHYSICS – is one of the major branches of science. People who work in physics
are called physicists.
Physicists study matter and the forces (pushes or pulls) that act on it.
(Matter is what makes up all physical objects.) Physicists also study many different
forms of energy.
The objects that physicists study range in size from the tiny building blocks of matter
to huge groups of stars

POLONIUM – a radioactive element discovered by Pierre and Marie Curie in 1898

RADIUM – a highly radioactive metallic element discovered by Pierre and Marie Curie
in 1898

RESEARCH – an investigation into a subject in order to discover or prove facts

SATURN – the sixth planet in line from the Sun and the second largest planet
in the solar system

SCHOLAR – a person who has good knowledge of a particular subject

SIGHT – perception of objects by use of the eyes. Or the image of things created by our eyes

SUNDIAL – an object that was used to tell time by the shadow position when placed under the sun

TESLA COIL – Tesla Coil is the most important invention of Nikola Tesla. It is an air-core machine that makes light. Tesla Coil was invented in 1891

THEORY OF EVOLUTION – the process by which the living things transform in order to adapt for existence

THEORY OF RELATIVITY – Albert's idea that say that it is impossible to know whether or not you are moving unless u can look at another object

THOMAS EDISON – was born February 11, 1847 in Milan, Ohio. He was one of the United States most well-known inventors

VACCINATION – the processes of receiving a shot at the doctor's office, by which you are given a version of the germ that is dead or very weak, so you body can learn to how to fight it

VENUS – is the second planet from the Sun and is the second brightest object in the night sky after the Moon

WIRELESS – (referring to a device) not using wires. Able to operate on electromagnetic waves, ex: radio, cell phone, etc

WORLD WAR – also known as the First World War, was a global war centered in Europe that began on 28th July 1914 and lasted until 11th November 1918

X-RAY – a form of electromagnetic radiation, similar to light but capable of going through a hard solid object and revealing the inside of it